Louis Kinney Harlow, Joel Cook

**An Isleboro Sketch**

Louis Kinney Harlow, Joel Cook

**An Isleboro Sketch**

ISBN/EAN: 9783744733489

Printed in Europe, USA, Canada, Australia, Japan

Cover: Foto ©Thomas Meinert / pixelio.de

More available books at **www.hansebooks.com**

# AN ISLESBORO SKETCH

By JOEL COOK.

WITH ILLUSTRATIONS BY LOUIS K. HARLOW.

PUBLISHED BY THE
BOSTON PHOTOGRAVURE CO.
1890.

# PENOBSCOT BAY.

From gray sea fog, from icy drift,
From peril and from pain,
The home-bound fisher greets thy lights,
O hundred-harbored Maine!

WHITTIER.

SAMUEL CHAMPLAIN, the intrepid French explorer and religious enthusiast, is believed to have been the first white man who sailed upon Penobscot Bay. Captain George Waymouth, who came after him in 1605, took possession for England and set up a cross upon its shores near where is now the city of Belfast. Waymouth marvelled at the magnificence of this wonderful bay with its broad, deep waters and great river, writing home that "many who had been travellers in sundry countries and in most famous rivers, affirmed them not comparable to this — the most beautiful, rich, large, secure harboring river that the world affordeth."

In those early days the region of the Penobscot was the semi-fabulous Norumbega, the Europeans knowing no river that was its equal, and no bay with such extensive surface and enormous tidal flow. Many were then the wondrous tales of weird Norumbega. The Penobscot is the greatest bay on the Maine coast, which in many respects is the most remarkable sea-coast in this country. Its jagged and uneven contour is seamed with deep inlets and serrated by craggy headlands projecting far out into the ocean, while between are hundreds of rocky and romantic islands. This grandest of Maine harbors, with its stern headlands and green archipelagoes, conducts to the ocean the largest of Maine's rivers.

The noble Penobscot was in early times the home of the war-like Tarratines, whose fame also went abroad as the remarkable people of this wonderful Norumbega. From its sources to the sea this river, which bears on its bosom the vast products of Maine's forests, is 175 miles long. Its embouchure broadens out into the enormous bay filled with islands, and the wedge shape of the lower river, by gathering such a vast flow of waters suddenly compressed at the Bucksport Narrows below Bangor, makes a rapidly rushing tide and an ebb and flow rising seventeen feet at Bangor.

The shores of this grand bay and river were part of the French Acadia, for the Frenchmen soon took this region away from England, and the powerful Tarratines became their firm friends through the influence of the Jesuit missionaries sent among them from Canada. These Indians named it Penobscot, meaning "where the land is covered with rocks," and their town on a narrow jutting peninsula on the eastern shore, was Pentagoet, or "the stream

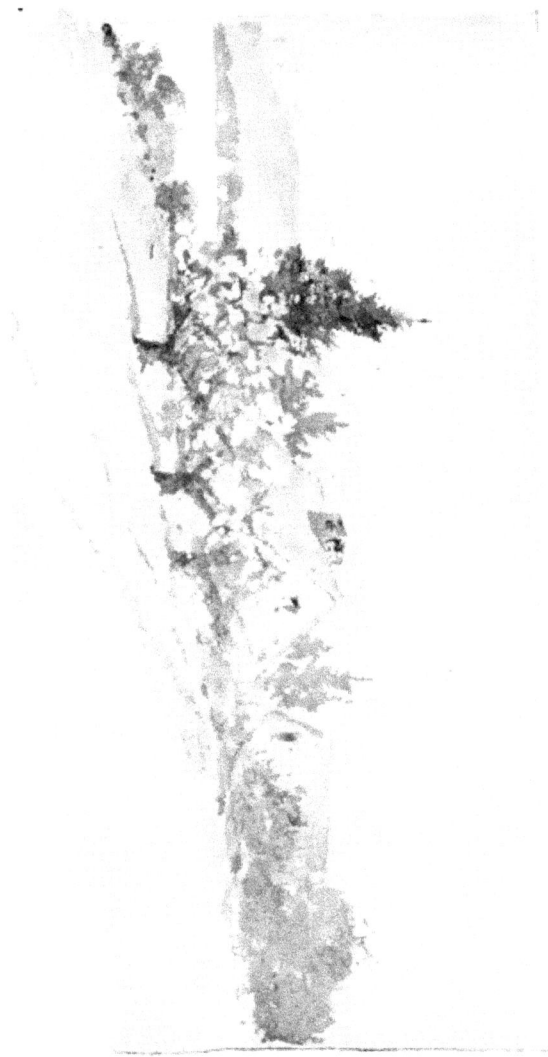

ON COOMB'S BLUFF.  No. Islesboro.

where there are rapids." The Plymouth Company first estab-
lished here an English trading post controlled from Massachusetts.
Then the French captured it and built Fort Pentagoet, long one
of their strongholds. The Dutch from New York took it; the
French recaptured it; and then becoming the noted town of Castine,
the English plundered and finally held it. This fortress of the
Penobscot, abounding with relics and scarred by repeated wars,
is now vegetating in the peaceful splendor of a popular watering
place.

The islands and shores of this extensive bay are covered with
forests — one of the crowning adornments of "hundred-harbored
Maine." The head-waters of the Penobscot traverse an immense
territory abounding with miles upon miles of the finest pine, spruce
and hemlock. Through these great woods of the primeval forest

the visitor penetrates in approaching the shores of the bay. Its bold western coast forms the well-known Maine counties of Knox and Waldo. Its abutting lands and islands were included in the "Muscongus Patent" which King George I. issued and which came to the Massachusetts Colonial Governor, Samuel Waldo, before the Revolution. This extensive patent embraced a tract thirty miles wide on each side of the Penobscot, and was a princely domain.

In those days in Boston, the Governor's grand-daughter visited a certain book-store so often that she became enamoured of the handsome young man behind the counter. The youthful book-seller

A SHORE RAVINE.
No. Islesboro

ALONG THE SHORE.

Coombs's Bluff.

was Henry Knox, afterwards one of Washington's most trusted generals. Their love had the usual ending, and the marriage ultimately made Knox the owner of the great domain, and the "patroon of Penobscot Bay." After the Revolution, he lived in baronial state in his palace at Thomaston, dispensing such princely hospitality that although he owned the best part of Maine he was literally "land poor," and became a bankrupt before he died. His descendants and successors have since divided up his extensive principality.

The most magnificent portion of General Knox's domain were the beautiful waters of Penobscot Bay and its many picturesque islands, whose graceful contours make the most attractive and capacious archipelago upon the Atlantic coast. The jutting point of Owl's Head guards the entrance to the bay on the western shore, and limestone and granite rocks environ the coast and islands. To the northward they rise into the tree-crowned and towering Camden mountains, boldly elevated far above the shore to cast grand shadows far across the bay as the afternoon sun sinks in the western sky to make most gorgeous sunsets.

Round-topped Megunticook stands 1400 feet above the little harbor at Camden and visitors often clamber to its top to get the grand view over the galaxy of sister peaks environing it, and across the broad blue bay and its splendid archipelago with the swelling peaks of distant Mount Desert far away to the eastward, and the limitless ocean seen beyond the southern entrance.

In front are spread out the islands in the centre of the great expanse of blue waters, deliciously nestling under the trees that fringe their upland slopes. Such is the view to-day over the most charming portion of France's prized Acadia — one of Nature's fairest scenes.

# ISLESBORO SCENERY.

A TTRACTIVE beyond all its other scenic beauties is the gem of Penobscot Bay, the "insular town of Islesboro," the chief of the five hundred or more islands dotted upon the magnificent waters of this grand interior sea. Islesboro, or Long Island, is an elongated strip of land in the centre of the charming bay, stretching some thirteen miles, and having on either side the mainland, distant from one to five miles, with much of the intervening water surface varied by islands. This long strip of Islesboro rises into highlands and is of varying widths, being deeply indented, and in three places almost bisected by ravines and fissures making beautiful bays and coves, where the gentle waters plash upon the pebbly beaches, fringing their sloping shores.

Bold banks rise above these bays, crowned with evergreens, and presenting the delightful pastoral landscape of field and hillside,

12

LILY POND.
HEAD OF SPRAGUES COVE.

water and woodland giving such charms to New England coast scenery. The lands are generally highest in the central parts, the hills and vales and wooded slopes giving perfect views. The long and narrow island covers about ten square miles of irregular contour, broadening or narrowing as the little harbors may indent it, while in many places the surface rises over a hundred feet into

SHORE TREES ON BEAUTY COVE. — CENTRAL ISLESBORO.

bold bluffs. The bracing air, come from what quarter it may, blows freely over the whole island, combining the healthful breezes of both mountain and sea, and making a miniature paradise.

This "insular town of Islesboro" was a famous hunting ground of the Tarratines, and remained in a state of nature until the first white men settled there in 1769. Twenty years later, including Seven Hundred Acre Island, Job's, Lassell's, Moose, Spruce, the two Ensigns and some other islands, it was incorporated into a town. About half the men are sea captains, and the rest farmers. Early history described this fortunate island as having "neither a rich man nor a poor man." All the land titles came down from the old patroon, General Knox, and there were any number of Pendletons, Coombs and Thomases, and old John Gilkey and Shubael Williams, whose descendants are yet living on their ancestral farms.

Islesboro has been one of those happy regions described by the seer, that has had little history. The British marauders in 1778 came over the bay from Castine and killed Gilkey's cows, while Shubael Williams proved too sturdy a patriot for them and was carried off and flogged. Again in 1813 the British captured a vessel on the bay, when a party from Islesboro put off in boats and within a few hours recaptured her. But the island has not had much history, though its people have looked out on many stirring events on Penobscot Bay. Once an Islesboro man murdered his wife and pleaded insanity, but the jury found him guilty, and he squared the account by killing himself in jail before the law hanged him.

In the various pleasant sketches in this little book, Mr. Harlow and Mr. Howe have given some idea of the many scenic beauties

HEAD OF SEAL HARBOR
CENTRAL ISLESBORO.

of Islesboro. The northern end of the island, from its contour, was not inappropriately called "Turtle Head" by one of the early visitors, the Colonial Governor Pownall of Massachusetts. Not far south from this head the beautiful little island inlet of Sprague's Cove is thrust far into the land, the entrance making a snug harbor, while above a pretty stream flows down through the trees, falling over an old mill-dam long since abandoned.

Upon the eastern shore Sabbath Day Harbor is indented, its abrupt northern banks rising into Coomb's Bluff. This bold promontory of beautiful contour is rounded in the centre, and has green pastures where contented sheep browse upon fields sloping off to the ponderous gray and red bordering cliffs. Many adornments are here, of dark firs and beeches, with the attractive arbor vitæ dotted about. Nestling among the trees are a few cottages of these farmer-fishermen giving picturesqueness to the scene.

These primitive people — naturally aquatic — will only cultivate a few acres around their homes, leaving the lands mainly to the sheep, while they tend their nets on the shores below, or sail off on a fishing-smack or coaster for a season's voyage. Like most of the "fishermen-farmers" of the coast of Maine, they are never busy, and always have plenty of time at disposal for gossip or bargaining. Seldom in a hurry, they dislike beginning any work until, in their parlance, they are "good and ready."

Coomb's Bluff gives an outlook over the eastern bay and its islands, with the distant shores and mountains, that is magnificent. The massive Blue Hill stands up an isolated guardian behind the pleasant white houses and church spire on the peninsula of Castine off to the northward. Those now pleasant waters have been at times red with the blood of some of the fiercest naval battles in American history. One might almost walk around this entire Bluff, on the topmost edge of its rocky walls, did it not occasionally break down into abrupt and deep ravines, sloping off to the clear pebbly beaches of the coves below. Scramble down a ravine and there little coves are found separated by bold promontories thrust into the sea, hollowed out but not overthrown by the waves. Far over the waters are beautiful views of the distant dots of sails, colored white or gray as sunlight or shadow may paint them, scattered for miles along the bay, or out on the distant ocean.

Old Shubael Williams, of Revolutionary memory, selected his farm on a lovely spot in the centre of the island, where two pairs of indenting bays have almost bisected the island and enclosed it. Several fine harbors environ this farm, among them Seal Harbor, enclosed by Keller's Point, a safe haven for the largest vessels, and Bounty Cove, and Crow Cove, their attractive shore lines presenting many scenic charms. After the old man had suffered for his sturdy patriotism, his pretty daughter became enamoured of a British soldier at Castine. He used to cross the bay to meet her clandestinely, but unfortunately he came once too often. Upon a cold night he skated over the ice, guided by a light in the cottage window, but just before reaching the shore he fell through an air-hole and was drowned. The father was not very sorry, but the daughter grieved sadly. Time, however, is a great assuager of grief — she afterwards married another.

To the southward is a most attractive haven, Gilkey's Harbor, on the western side of Islesboro, formed by the enclosing shores of several adjacent islands. Here also the largest ships can safely anchor in all weathers. These pretty islets enclose an almost completely landlocked sheet of water, where the pleasures of the sailing yacht and smallest row-boat can be enjoyed in perfect

security. This miniature summer sea, bounded by rocky forest-covered shores, with an occasional old-fashioned farm-house on the upland, rivals in its sylvan and aquatic beauties the world-famous Loch Katrine or Lake Windermere.

One primitive farm-house on the sloping shore, elevated nearly a hundred feet above the water, and standing about a thousand feet back, is particularly attractive. The admiring observer is puzzled to decide which view is the prettiest, that from the harbor looking ashore, or the splendid picture of land and water loveliness over Gilkey's Harbor and the western bay. The greensward stretches down to the water. The placid harbor is in front, having the elongated projection of Grindle's Point encircling it, and a little white light-house at the entrance. Spread in front as the harbor stretches two or three miles southward is the archipelago of protecting islands. Outside glistens the broad Penobscot Bay with its grand western background of the Camden Mountains, their line of rounded peaks of nearer green or more distant blue, over which the cloud shadows are chasing, running off far away towards Belfast. The surrounding islands and the smooth and placid waters within their embrace, make as fair a harbor as one could hope to see; while the distant mountains form a noble setting for the gem.

# AN ISLESBORO LEGEND.

THE region surrounding Islesboro was in the olden time the home of the warlike Tarratines, who had our pleasant island for their favorite hunting ground. These Indians were a branch of the fierce Abenaqui nation, and the French who came to Acadia early wished to convert this powerful tribe to Christianity. Among the French noblemen who were sent out in the seventeenth century, coming with his regiment, was Vincent, Baron de St. Castine, Lord of Oleron in the Pyrenees. Inspired by a chivalrous desire to spread the Catholic faith among these Indians, he visited them in 1667. As Longfellow tells it:

> "Baron Castine of St. Castine
> Has left his Chateau in the Pyrenees,
> And sailed across the western seas."

The grand Sachem of the Tarratines was Madockawando, who then ruled in the fabled land of Norumbega, of which Europeans

A SHORE FARM ON DICKEY'S HARBOR

had heard so much that was marvellous. The Baron came and
tarried, soon finding warm friends among these children of the
forest. As in Virginia, the Sachem had a susceptible daughter,
and this dusky Pocahontas of the Penobscot, captivated by the
courtly graces of the young and handsome Baron, fell in love
with him :

> For man is fire, and woman is tow,
> And the Somebody comes and begins to blow.

The usual result followed, so that it was not long before —

> Lo! the young Baron of St. Castine,
> Swift as the wind is, and as wild,
> Has married the dusky Tarratine,
> Has married Madockawando's child!

This marriage made him a member of the tribe, and he soon
advanced to leadership.

The restless and warlike Indians almost worshipped the chivalrous young Frenchman, who was their apostle, and became their
chieftain and led them in repeated raids against their English and
Indian foes. But he ultimately tired of this roving life and returned
to "his Chateau in the Pyrenees," taking his Indian bride along.
Then marvelled much his French tenantry :

> Down in the village day by day
> The people gossip in their way,
> And stare to see the Baroness pass
> On Sunday morning to early Mass;
> And when she kneeleth down to pray,
> They wonder, and whisper together, and say
> "Surely this is no heathen lass'"

And in course of time they learn to bless
The Baron and the Baroness.
And in the course of time the Curate learns
A secret so dreadful that by turns
He is ice and fire, he freezes and burns.
The Baron at confession hath said,
    That though this woman be his wife,
He hath wed her as the Indians wed —
    He hath bought her for a gun and a knife!

This caused much trouble, but the Curate finally managed to make all things right through the efficacy of a Christian wedding.

The choir is singing the matin song,
    The doors of the church are opened wide;
The people crowd, and press, and throng,
    To see the bridegroom and the bride.
They enter and pass along the nave;
They stand upon the father's grave;

The bells are ringing soft and slow;
The living above and the dead below
Give their blessing on one and twain;
The warm wind blows from the hills of Spain,
The birds are building, the leaves are green,
And Baron Castine of St. Castine,
Hath come at last to his own again.

The son of this Baron by his Tarratine princess, became the chief of the tribe and ruled it until, in 1721, he was captured in an English raid and taken prisoner to Boston. He is described as brave and magnanimous, and when brought before the Puritan Council at Boston for trial, he wore his French uniform, and was accused of attending an Abenaqui Council fire. He replied with spirit: "I am an Abenaquis by my mother; all my life has been passed among the nation that has made me chief and commander over it. I could not be absent from a council where the interests of my brethren were to be discussed. The dress I now wear is one becoming my rank and birth as an officer of the Most Christian King of France, my master."

He was held several months as a prisoner, but was ultimately released. Finally he, too, returned to the ancestral chateau in the Pyrenees. His lineal descendants are said to yet rule the Abenaqui nation, but it has dwindled almost to nothingness. Honoring these memories Fort Pentagoet became Castine. In and around its harbor and along the shores of Islesboro, in the many wars this region has seen, there have been fought no less than five important naval battles, and relics of these bitter conflicts are yet found.

All the Abenaqui tribes were firm allies of the Americans during the Revolution. For their fealty they were given an extensive reservation where their remnants now live, on Indian Island in the Penobscot at Oldtown above Bangor. Catching fish and rafting logs are now the occupations of the descendants of the great Indian race of Norumbega.

# ISLESBORO INN.

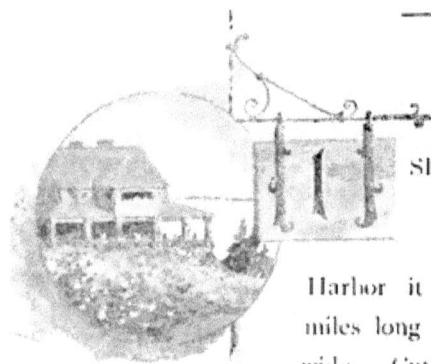

SLESBORO beauties expand as one goes further southward over the pleasant island. Below Gilkey's Harbor it narrows to a bold ridge several miles long and seldom more than a half-mile wide. Cut deeply into this ridge is another of those bisecting narrows where that picturesque little haven, Dark Harbor, is thrust abruptly in among the cliffs of the eastern shore, broadening out inside the rocky walls that guard the entrance. It is almost hidden from view when out on the bay, and the over-hanging trees, combined with the thorough enclosure of this be-witching little basin, produce the delicious shade that has named it the Dark Harbor.

The head waters of this pleasant bay are dammed, forming a basin of about a dozen acres. This beautiful lake is enclosed by

sloping shores, wooded sometimes to the water's edge, and having interspersed diminutive beaches, or small projecting rocks. Over it is thrown a foot bridge, beyond which winding steps upon the southern bank ascend the cliff to a lovely grove of spruce trees, the ground beneath them carpeted with gray moss, while moss also covers many of the tree-trunks. This charming spot is Dark Harbor Head, and a short walk upon a woodland path brings you out of the grove to still higher open land, upon the elevated part of which is built the rustic and comfortable Islesboro Inn.

There cannot be found upon the rocky and romantic coast of Maine a more attractive location. From its western front there are a series of splendid glimpses over Gilkey's Harbor and the western bay and islands to the bold background of the Camden mountains. From the eastern front is seen the grand sweep of East Penobscot bay, its broad surface bearing distant and scattered islands, with the hilly wooded shores of Cape Rosier across the water, and to the south again in the far distance rise the bisected round-topped peaks of Mount Desert, thirty miles away. To the southward are the group of Fox Islands with North Haven and Vinal Haven, while off through a bewitching vista among them looms up the Isle au Haut, their outer guardian upon the ocean's edge. The bold and graceful outline of Southern Islesboro bounds the view in that direction.

Such is the gorgeous scene from the Islesboro Inn, over the East Penobscot bay as scores of delicate white-winged yachts, standing over before the strength of a fresh northwestern breeze, are threading the mazy thoroughfares among these pleasant islands and dancing upon the sparkling waves on their various courses through the bay

ALONG THE EAST SHORE.

SOUTH ISLESBORO.

or to Mount Desert and the further eastern havens. Strolling further
along the Islesboro grounds one enters more beautiful woodland
groves. The smooth gray-trunked beeches have openings among
their groups showing glimpses of the water. There are spreading
maples and white birches; and across the grassy openings the dark
spruces form a sharp contrast with the gnarled and fantastic trunks
of the arbor vitæ, while the tall ash and yellow birch stand apart
in native dignity. And everywhere it seems as if this charming
island were planted with groups of gorgeous Christmas trees —
millions of them, growing stately and symmetrical, and beautiful
beyond description in their native and vigourous glory upon these
rocky hills. Lowly, yet lovely, there also grow in many shaded
nooks, acres of ferns of attractive forms and most delicate texture.

The visitor may admire the beautiful in nature, but an essential
element to its thorough enjoyment is to have at the same time
complete personal comfort. The graceful and elegant Islesboro Inn
seems to have grown naturally into the charms of its environment.
It is simple and homelike both outside and inside and impresses
one as being constructed more like a handsome and comfortable
private rural residence than a hostelrie. Standing upon a beautiful
promontory with most attractive surroundings, the architecture to be
in thorough keeping is unique, and the opposite of the four-story
barn-like rectangular caravansary usually seen at a fashionable
summer resort. The structure is low and somewhat long, with a
tasteful roof outline that is broken into several large gambrels,
with stucco faces, wooden cross beams and latticed windows.

This building is constructed after a familiar type of English

A GLIMPSE OF GILKEY'S HARBOR FROM THE ISLESBORO INN, LOOKING WEST

country-house, and is broadened at the base by spreading verandahs
within heavy stone arches. The internal finish and arrangements
are handsome but simple, without the slightest indication of dreari-
ness. There are no waste places in the form of large rooms,
and the parlors, halls and smoking room, both in size and furnishing,
give a solid impression of comfort. The cuisine and service are
closely in character with the building. Nominally an Inn, the place
is in character more a private club, having accommodation for
perhaps forty or fifty people.

The dining hall, the one large apartment in the Inn, is admir-
ably situated, its broad, plate-glass windows having, on either side,
charming views over the East and West Penobscot bays. On the
one hand the broad water glints in the sunlight as the visitor pauses
at his breakfast to look far away at the distant blue outlines of
Mount Desert and the Blue Hill. On the other side, seen through
trees in lovely natural groupings, and across green slopes, are glimpses
of the sheltered waters of Gilkey's Harbor, nestling within its enclosure of islands, the distant bay and mountains guarding the
western horizon. Under the broad stone piazza arches, as one
looks out, are thus framed a series of lovely pictures.

The natural surroundings of the Inn are charming. The fasci-
nating little basin of Dark Harbor, deep down among the tree-
covered cliffs, is but a short distance away. Running up into the
land nearly a half-mile, this oval lake almost cuts the island in
twain, only a narrow neck of land dividing it from Gilkey's Harbor
on the other side. There are floating wharves with pleasant sail
and rowboats ready to start in any direction over the waters of the

GULL POINT.
EAST SHORE FROM THE ISLESBORO INN. LOOKING SOUTH.

bay. The enclosed basin inside the dam is flooded at high tide, and, warmed by the sun, gives opportunity for salt water bathing. In several places on the rocky shores near the Inn, limpid springs of the clearest water bubble out of the cliffs. It was in the very centre of the now enclosed Dark Harbor basin, where she had taken refuge, that the first iron steam propeller ever constructed — the Bangor — was burnt in August, 1845.

The peninsula making the southern extremity of Islesboro is a pleasant ridge of highlands about two miles long, elevated in the centre and sloping either way to the water. It abounds in attractive woodland rambles remarkable for their sylvan beauties. A short distance from the Inn on the western verge of this peninsula another boating station is located for the convenience of aquatic exploration about the smooth waters and varied coasts enclosing Gilkey's Harbor.

THE ISLESBORO INN

Here is a grand inland and protected expanse of water for rowing or sailing, as safe from wind and wave as the smoothest lake. Islesboro Inn is in close communication with a dozen of the most interesting localities on Penobscot bay. A few miles away, on the western coast, is Camden, with its picturesque harbor, its lakes and mountains. Belfast, upon its deep bay, is to the northward, with Bucksport and Bangor beyond. Over on the southeastern side of Islesboro, and a half-dozen miles off, is the numerous archipelago of the Fox Islands, the many rocky and wooded islets being divided by intricate passages disclosing varied and sometimes grotesque shapes among the bordering cliffs. Castine is to the northeast; and nearer to the eastward over the bay are the rocky shores and rolling wooded hills of Cape Rosier. Breaking into the northern shore of the Fox Island group is the picturesque little haven known as Pulpit Harbor.

The native people of this primitive island live in neat houses with broad fronts that are usually painted white, and the men being chiefly sea captains, their cottage front doors naturally open upon steep stairways, rising almost straight up to the higher floors, like a ship's companion ladder. They are living to-day just as their ancestors have done for generations, knowing little and caring less in their secluded elysium of what is passing outside. Upon the pebbly beaches, shells and sea-urchins are found, while fish-hawks and gulls circle about and scream above our heads. Scattered over this pleasant region are the little white-tombed graveyards where rest the forefathers of the island. It is one of the fairest scenes in nature, only just discovered by the fashionable world, and is destined

to be among the most famous resorts of the American coast.　Such is the gem of Penobscot bay, the "insular town of Islesboro."

> Wert thou all that I wish thee, great, glorious and free,
> First flower of the earth and first gem of the sea.
>
> Tom Moore.

"AN ISLAND INLET."
Head of Spragues Cove, NORTH ISLESBORO.

A TURN IN THE ROAD NEAR THE ISLESBORO INN

www.ingramcontent.com/pod-product-compliance
Lightning Source LLC
Chambersburg PA
CBHW021641270326
41931CB00008B/1105